TEXTUI

SUE LEWIS

Cinnamon Press
:: small miracles from distinctive voices ::

Published by Cinnamon Press
Meirion House
Tanygrisiau
Blaenau Ffestiniog
Gwynedd, LL41 3SU
www.cinnamonpress.com

Designed and typeset in Palatino by Cinnamon Press.
Cover design by Adam Craig.
Cinnamon Press is represented in the UK by Inpress Ltd and in Wales by the Books Council of Wales.

Acknowledgements

'Fabric' was first published in *The Fenland Reed*, Issue 2: Spring 2016.

'Ostinato' appeared in a different version (as Dal Segno al Fine) in *Morley Magazine*, Volume 124 No 1 Spring/Summer 2018.

'Kenosis' and 'Overheard' were first published in *South Bank Poetry* Issue 31.

'Shift' was shortlisted in the Morley Arts Festival Poetry Competition July 2018. (Judged by Inua Ellams).

Thank you to all the people who have helped me on my poetry journey, especially Peter Evans, Rachel Sambrooks, Rebecca Hubbard, Helen Eastman and Katherine Lockton.

I am deeply indebted to Jan Fortune for her inspiration and for Ty'n y Coed, where it all began.

Contents

For my sister, Helen. Always and for ever.

Texture

Fabric

So many years
in the weaving.

You were crafted,
stitched to a pattern,
embroidered for effect.

But when you understand
that the way forward
is the way back

and the question
is, in fact,
the answer

then

in the unravelling,
the unpicking
and the casting off

you will surely find
your gold threads
and your silver threads:

hold fast to these.
Discard the rest.

Ostinato

Each day, it seems, a part of me turns up.

Don't act surprised. This is what healing brings:
some motif in the music finds me out.
I pick up threads forgotten long ago
and start to weave them into shape again.

I retrace paths and keep a steady beat,
past tender crocus rising from the earth:
bright half-notes clustering on fragile stems.
They keep on coming back. I thought they'd gone.

The daylight lengthens; winter turns to spring
and there's the zest of sharp new green. Observe
the sky. I taste this sweet song on my tongue,
then dance its rhythm out. March madness, brief.

The music fills my head. Forgive my bliss.

Kenosis

Helen: I went everywhere,
tried to make amends. I offered incense
to the Buddha and Guan-yin, slipped silent
into empty churches, sat alone in
tall cathedrals with their jewelled windows,
whispering floors. Stooped and lit so many
tiny candles for you, Helen, fumbling and inept.
Small flames were trembling smoky-yellow
throughout England. Other places too:
Jerusalem—the Wailing Wall—I stood
like an impostor with the women dressed in black
and pushed my scribbled prayer into the rock.
The Holy Sepulchre, I queued for half an hour
to kiss what must be kissed, then, dizzy,
went outside and breathed the sunlight in.
Oh please, God. Please.
It made no difference.
The only answer to a prayer
is something we've already guessed.

Folded

I cannot bear the waiting.
Day is folded into dark,
night is shaken out
and held up to the light.
Morning rips me open once again:
I gather up each threadbare shred,
construct a prayer flag of hope.
The circus act of birds goes on:
quick sparrows squabble in the hedge.
Pigeons chant soft hymns for you.
All this stopped week, I watch for signs.
Rose petals scatter like a blessing.

Codicil

Burn me,
you said.
Bear my ashes
to the sacred river.
Burn me.

Join me
with the flowing water.

Haul my longship
to the cold North Sea.
Drag it, groaning,
to the grey salt tide.

Loose the smouldering arrow:
start the fire.

While the prey-birds circle,
drench my pyre with
precious oils and

let me
blaze once more.

Survivors

Don't pity us. We're not like you.
We've been to the abyss; looked down.
We know things you don't know.
Often we will recognise each other
for we're missing our thick skins:
not useful, in the end.

We've served our time.
Counted out new moons.
A day came when we
opened up our fragile windows,
let the birdsong pierce us.
Set a course for Ithaca again.

We cover our stigmata now
and talk amongst ourselves.
Can't find the words to share this
because you wouldn't understand.
Don't pity us. We're back.
We've risen from our ashes.

Shift

Our bright world rusts:
fine fragments fall.

Time tramples, livid,
to a pulse of ancient anger
but we tell ourselves
this too will pass.

There'll be some shift;
some circularity to bring us peace.

We watch for messages:
stars burn, clouds burst,
fresh rain veins down the glass.

That split of rainbow light
which hurts the eyes, the colours
dazzling, jewel-hued:

each time it happens
we're disarmed by joy.

Change

We walk down to the tree-line,
past the half-shy ponies, watching.
Soon this will be dense with green.
But, as it is, the trees
are still a charcoal sketch,
a smudge rubbed with a cautious thumb;
a touch of purplish chalk highlighting
faith in growth, pre-figuring that
imminent leaf-burst.
And then we come to water,
sliding over granite rocks.
The sudden sunlight turns it
molten pewter, gleaming.
We can taste it,
that austere, abundant life.

Abrasion

New pencils stutter
when they're sharp
as if they're baulking
at the white expanse.
That effort to begin the line.
Don't be alarmed.
Mistakes can be unmade.
Persist.
They will ameliorate
as they begin to flow
staccato to *legato*.
Resistance melts with use
but, should they go too far,
it's easy to restore the edge.

Unbroken

water
inkstone

softly circle
soot black stick

scent of cedar
hush of rain

wait slow
transformation

thirsty brush
the untouched page

concentrate
the black ink flows

not speaking
everything is said

sacred life force
of the written word

Rearview

Lean-faced street dog
snaps at its fleas.
On the platform
a man sleeps deeply
on a cardboard sheet.

We climb from the train at Chandigarh
into hazed light and pink dust.
Stunned by noise and movement,
searing colour, deafening heat.

Everything is cracked and broken
under the sun's oven.
We pick our way past beggars, traders.
There is rubbish everywhere.

We slide into air-conditioned cars
and, grateful, close the door.
I catch our driver's dark eye
unguarded in the mirror:

the shock of his contempt.

Banished

We're the last group of the afternoon.
The sun is almost banished
to a faint stain on the courtyard
as we scramble up the steps
and swarm the dark interior.

There, the child-sized bed where a
Dalai Lama once slept, dreaming.

We hurry past the towering stupas,
squeeze around the beaming Buddhas
while an old monk calmly
closes up the rooms behind us:
fits the heavy wooden doors.

Our guide has words prepared for us about
'the peaceful liberation of Tibet'.
There's a train all the way now:
from Beijing to Lhasa.

Released again, outside,
we gulp the high, thin air
and, in the sun's slow fade,
we take pictures of ourselves.

Le Saut dans le Vide

So. Lunch she says.
I set off early, train to Crystal Palace,
then the 3 (which goes to Regent Street).
I check my phone. The sun comes out. The bus fills up.
I used to drive through here: she's lived round here so long,
since art school at the LCC. The leap into the void.

I have to ask: which stop? Then walk to Dulwich Picture Gallery,
queue up in the Café for a table. People try to push
their way ahead. But I'm a Londoner. I know
to keep my elbows sharp. And here she is. She's full of life.
She's in her Lycra leggings: been climbing on a wall in Bermondsey.
Of course she has. Her hair is dirty-blonde. She's beautiful. Says:
Mum! You've cut your hair? It's good.

We order cider, grilled halloumi salad, couscous. Cake.
Flat whites. Our elbows on the table, close, the sunlight seeping:
clatter of the cutlery, sweet hum of conversation. Buzz.

So now. She tells me of the trip she made to Liverpool to see
the work of Klein. Explains the theory of International Blue.
I tell her that they made a ballet of the *Tree of Codes*. Was sold out every night.
She laughs. That takes me back, she says. God, what a nightmare to proof-read.
A book of holes.

Overheard

Sweet cinnamon and cloves
the Rhine's broad sweep
the Altstadt after dark: those
fur coats on the midnight tram
a dozen roses, scarlet.

Yes. I tried to learn it.
But I couldn't trust a language
which insists the moon is masculine.

Ich kann kein Deutsch sprechen
and I can't go back there now.

It wasn't just the moon.

Moth

Small moth on my tablecloth
you're out of place: a piece of bark
that doesn't fit with knives and forks.
A silver smudge of nondescript
which, craving brilliance from the night,
goes circling round the burning glass
all pulsing air and beating flight
till, dizzy with the frantic dance,
exhausted, drops to rest between
my supper plate, my glass of wine,
with trembling wings. I understand.
I, too, am drawn towards the shine.

Liminal

Come to the doorway:
there's the strangest sky. Almost
evening: mesmerising brightness.

Stand there as the light fades:
time to step across.
Accept the chthonic invitation.

You have felt this resonance before:
swimming up from felted sleep,
flying through the mantra of the birds.

Green night waits to ripen
underneath the antique silver.
White scent of jessamine.

Lightning Source UK Ltd.
Milton Keynes UK
UKHW011937040220
358156UK00002B/116